REMEMBER MIRANDA

It is Cathy Wilson's first job. She is going to live with the Harvey family, and look after the two young children and the house. Cathy's parents are dead, and she has no brothers or sisters. She wants to be happy in her new home, but she is sometimes lonely. Duncan, the children's father, is often away in London. Cathy likes the children and she likes old Mrs Harvey, Duncan's mother, but she has no friends.

Of course, there is Nick, the farmer who lives across the fields. He has very blue eyes, and a warm, friendly smile. But it is not easy to be friendly with Nick, because Duncan hates him, and old Mrs Harvey gets angry when Cathy goes to dinner with Nick.

But why does Duncan hate Nick? Why does Nick tell Cathy to be careful at Beach House? And why does nobody want to talk about Miranda, the children's mother, who died two years ago? There are a lot of secrets in the Harvey family, and Cathy begins to ask questions.

Soon she begins to find the answers. And she learns why everybody remembers Miranda . . .

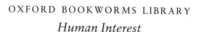

OXFORD BOOKWORMS LIBRARY
Human Interest

Remember Miranda

Stage 1 (400 headwords)

Series Editor: Jennifer Bassett
Founder Editor: Tricia Hedge
Activities Editors: Jennifer Bassett and Alison Baxter

ROWENA AKINYEMI

Remember Miranda

OXFORD UNIVERSITY PRESS

OXFORD
UNIVERSITY PRESS

Great Clarendon Street, Oxford OX2 6DP

Oxford University Press is a department of the University of Oxford.
It furthers the University's objective of excellence in research, scholarship,
and education by publishing worldwide in

Oxford New York

Auckland Cape Town Dar es Salaam Hong Kong Karachi
Kuala Lumpur Madrid Melbourne Mexico City Nairobi
New Delhi Shanghai Taipei Toronto

With offices in

Argentina Austria Brazil Chile Czech Republic France Greece
Guatemala Hungary Italy Japan Poland Portugal Singapore
South Korea Switzerland Thailand Turkey Ukraine Vietnam

OXFORD and OXFORD ENGLISH are registered trade marks of
Oxford University Press in the UK and in certain other countries

ISBN 978 0 19 478918 9

A complete recording of this Bookworms edition of
Remember Miranda is available on audio CD ISBN 978 0 19 478853 3

Typeset by Wyvern Typesetting Ltd, Bristol

Printed in China

Illustrated by: Tracy Rich

Word count (main text): 5060 words

For more information on the Oxford Bookworms Library,
visit www.oup.com/bookworms

CONTENTS

1

Beach House

The children and their father remember Miranda, of course, and they talk about her sometimes. Miranda's sister often visits us, and she always tells the children a story about their mother. Nick remembers Miranda; I know he does. And in the hospital, Grandma remembers, too. They all remember Miranda.

I never met Miranda, but every day I look at her photograph, next to the telephone in the kitchen, the picture of her with her children. Every day I look at her beautiful dark eyes and her long dark hair.

I first saw Miranda's photograph two years ago. It was a cold October day, and I left London for my new job with a family in Norfolk. I drove north, past Norwich, and it began to rain. It was dark and there was a strong wind so

It began to rain.

I drove slowly and carefully. I wanted to see the Harvey children before they went to bed. But because of the weather, it was eight o'clock before I arrived in Cromer. I drove through the town, along the sea road.

Suddenly, I stopped. There was a tree across the road. I got out of my car. It was a big tree, and I couldn't move it.

'What's the matter?'

Just then, a car drove up behind me and a man got out.

'What's the matter? Oh – a tree across the road.' He was a tall man, about thirty years old. 'Where are you going?' he asked.

'Not far,' I said. 'It's a house along this road, near the sea. It's called Beach House.'

'Oh, I know Beach House,' the man said. 'It's the last house along this road. But you can't drive there tonight, with this tree across the road.' He stopped for a minute. 'I'm Nick Watson, and I live at the farm along the road. We can go back to my house, and then walk across the fields to Beach House. Are you visiting for the weekend?'

'No, no. I'm going to work in the house and look after Mr Harvey's children. Their mother died two years ago, and their grandmother has arthritis in her legs and can't walk much now. So I'm going to look after the children and the house,' I told him. 'I met old Mrs Harvey in London, six weeks ago, and she gave me the job. Do you know the Harveys?'

The man laughed. His laugh was warm and friendly. 'Oh, yes, I know them,' he said.

We drove back down the road and into the farm. Then we walked across the fields. It was dark and windy and cold. After ten minutes we arrived at a big white house. The lights were on downstairs, and the house looked friendly. I had no home because my mother and father died

3

a long time ago, and I had no brothers or sisters. This was my first job and I wanted to be happy in this house.

A man opened the door. He looked tired and there was no smile on his face.

'Hello, I'm Cathy Wilson,' I began. 'I'm very late, I know. It's because the weather's so bad.'

'There's a tree down across the road,' Nick said. 'So Cathy left her car at the farm and we walked here.'

Duncan Harvey looked at Nick. 'You always want to help,' he said coldly. 'And you're always there at the right time, ready to help.' His face was angry and I didn't understand why.

'The wind's very strong . . .' I began.

'It doesn't matter,' Nick said. He smiled at me and his eyes were very blue. 'Goodbye, Cathy. Come and get your car tomorrow.'

Duncan said nothing. I went into the house and he took me through into the kitchen.

'Mother, here's Cathy,' he said.

Old Mrs Harvey sat near the window. 'Hello, my dear,' she said warmly. 'What a wind! Come and have something to eat.' She stood up and walked slowly across the room. Her hair was white, and she had a stick because of her bad legs.

I sat down and began to eat.

'Duncan is angry because he doesn't like Nick,' Mrs

4

'*You always want to help.*'

Harvey told me quietly. 'He's not angry with you.'

Why didn't Duncan like Nick? I thought. I didn't understand, but I didn't like to ask Mrs Harvey.

The next morning I met the children. Tim was five years old. He ran up and down the garden with a football. Susan was seven years old, a quiet little girl with big brown eyes. She watched me carefully but she didn't smile.

The weather changed and the sun was warm. In the afternoon I walked with the children by the sea. The sky was blue and the sea was beautiful. I cooked dinner and we all ate in the kitchen.

After dinner Juliet arrived.

'I left my car at Nick's,' she said. 'There's a tree across the road.' Juliet had long black hair and dark eyes. She was Miranda's sister.

'Miranda was wonderful,' she told me. 'Wonderful and beautiful.'

'Yes, I know,' I said quietly. 'I saw the photograph of her, next to the telephone, with Tim and Susan.'

'Miranda is our mummy,' Susan said. 'She died a long time ago.'

'Let's go to the cinema,' Juliet said suddenly. 'I want to take Susan and Tim. Cathy, you come with us.'

Tim began to shout. 'Let's go to the cinema! Let's go to the cinema!'

'Be quiet, Tim!' Duncan said. He looked angry. 'No,

'Be quiet, Tim!' Duncan said.

Juliet. It's school tomorrow, and the children must go to
bed early.'

Tim began to cry. 'I want to go with Juliet,' he said.

'No, Tim,' Duncan said.

'We can go to the cinema next weekend,' I said quickly.

'Let's play with your little cars now.' And soon Tim stopped crying.

The days went quickly. Duncan went to stay in London for three weeks for his work. He had a job with a big London company. He often worked on his computer at home, but he went away a lot, too. I liked the children and I liked old Mrs Harvey, but I had no friends.

One day, I came out of a shop in Cromer, and there was Juliet!

'Hello!' she said. 'It's good to see you! Let's go and have a coffee, and we can talk.'

And we did. Juliet told me about her teaching job, and she talked about Susan and Tim, and she talked about her sister.

'I often visited Miranda at Beach House because she wasn't happy there,' Juliet said quietly. 'Duncan is a difficult man; you can see that. He loved her, of course, but he was often away in London. She loved the children, and Grandma, but she was very lonely.'

I was lonely, too, at Beach House.

Juliet stood up and smiled warmly. 'I must go now. Let's go to the cinema this weekend with the children. Ask Grandma tonight, and ring me.'

And so I found a friend.

2

The first secret

The weather changed, and that autumn was warm and beautiful. Nearly every day I walked with the children along the beach. The sea was blue and friendly, and the trees, with their red and yellow autumn colours, looked beautiful in the sunlight. One afternoon we walked across the field and down the hill to the beach. Susan ran in front of Tim. They sang and laughed because they liked playing on the beach.

'Hello, Cathy. How are you?' someone said behind me.

'Hello, Cathy. How are you?'

I stopped. It was Nick, the tall farmer with the blue eyes. 'I'm well, thank you.'

'You look lonely,' he said, and smiled. 'You need some friends. Shall we meet in Cromer one day and have dinner?'

And so the next evening I drove to Nick's farm and we went into Cromer for dinner, and then we walked through the town to the gardens near the beach. I liked Nick. He was friendly and interesting. We didn't talk about the Harvey family all evening.

But before we said goodnight, Nick asked about Duncan. 'Are you going to tell Duncan about this evening?'

'No,' I said quickly. Then I stopped. 'Duncan is in London this month,' I went on slowly. 'Mrs Harvey told me – you and Duncan . . .'

Nick laughed quietly. 'So you have a secret now,' he said. 'Be careful, Cathy, at Beach House.'

'I don't understand,' I said. 'Why don't you like Duncan?'

'I can't talk about it,' Nick said.

I didn't tell Mrs Harvey about Nick, and perhaps that was wrong. But I did tell Juliet.

'I like Nick very much,' I told her. 'I want to see him again.' But Juliet was quiet and didn't talk much that afternoon.

That evening I put the children to bed and read them a story. Then I went slowly downstairs. I thought about

'Be careful, Cathy, at Beach House.'

Nick. I wanted to see him again.

Mrs Harvey sat quietly in her big chair in the kitchen. 'Cathy, I must talk to you, my dear,' she said. 'Come and sit down here.'

I sat down near her. I didn't want to talk – I wanted to finish my work in the kitchen and go upstairs to watch TV in my room.

'You're a good girl,' Mrs Harvey began kindly. 'Susan and Tim like you, and I'm very happy with your work in the house.'

I smiled, and waited for the 'but'. It arrived immediately.

'But I must talk to you about Nick Watson. Perhaps you are lonely here, with the children and me. Duncan is very quiet, I know that, and he's in London much of the time. But Nick doesn't like Duncan, and Duncan hates Nick. It's a long story and I don't want to talk about it. I'm not going to tell Duncan about your evening with Nick, but I don't want you to see Nick again.'

My face felt hot and my hands felt cold. Mrs Harvey knew about my dinner with Nick! Who told her? And why? I felt angry with Mrs Harvey because I wanted to see Nick again. But I didn't want to lose my job.

'I don't understand,' I began quietly.

Mrs Harvey stood up. 'Why must you understand?' she asked angrily. 'Don't see Nick Watson again! Do you hear me?'

'Come and sit down here.'

'No, Tim!' Mrs Harvey shouted.

'Grandma!'

We looked up, and saw Susan and Tim on the stairs. 'Children! What are you doing!' Mrs Harvey said. She took her stick and began to walk slowly across the room.

'Tim was afraid,' Susan said. 'He couldn't sleep, and so we came to call Cathy.'

'I wasn't afraid – *you* were afraid, because of Nick,' Tim said, and he pushed Susan.

'No, Tim!' Mrs Harvey shouted. Her face went white. 'Don't do that! Cathy, please go upstairs and put them back to bed.'

I ran upstairs and took the children back to their room. Tim put his little hands on my face and kissed me. 'Goodnight, Cathy,' he said. 'I like you.'

I smiled. 'I like you, too,' I said.

I said goodnight to Susan. 'I don't want Grandma to be angry with you,' she said quietly.

'Why are you afraid of Nick?' I asked.

'I don't know,' Susan said. 'Daddy hates him, but I don't know why.'

'He's a bad man,' Tim said. 'Grandma told me.'

And so I didn't see Nick again for a long time.

3

A terrible accident

Duncan came back and worked at home again. Why did he hate Nick? I wanted to understand, but I couldn't ask because I was a little afraid of Duncan. He didn't talk much and he worked for hours in his room.

Old Mrs Harvey liked to cook, but because of her arthritis she couldn't cook much and she couldn't look after the children and the house. She often felt upset because of this. But she was much happier with Duncan at home. She smiled more and she cooked breakfast for him nearly every

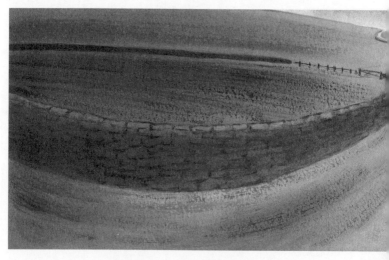

'Cathy! Are you all right?'

day. Sometimes she made bread. Duncan was kind to his mother and he played with the children every day. He drove them to school every morning and I drove them home in the afternoons.

One Friday afternoon I drove away from Beach House past Nick's farm. Just then, I saw Nick's Landrover on the farm road. 'He's driving very fast,' I thought. 'Oh no! He's not going to stop –' And he didn't. He drove out of the farm road and very nearly hit my car. I couldn't stop, so I drove off the road and the Landrover went past, only centimetres away.

The Landrover stopped. Nick got out, ran back to my car, and opened the door. 'Cathy! Are you all right?'

Then I saw a girl in the Landrover. It was Juliet. She got out and came up to us.

'You must drive more carefully, Nick!' she said angrily. 'You nearly hit Cathy then.' She wore a beautiful red coat

'*We don't want more accidents,*' *Juliet said quietly.*
'*Remember Miranda.*'

18

and black trousers. Her dark eyes were angry, but they looked at Nick and not at me.

'Cathy's all right,' he said to her. He put his hand on her arm. His blue eyes were kind, but they looked at Juliet and not at me.

'We don't want more accidents,' Juliet said quietly. 'Remember Miranda.'

'Please move your Landrover,' I said coldly. 'I must get to school for the children. I'm going to be late.'

'Don't be angry.' Nick smiled at me. 'I'm very sorry.' He got back into the Landrover and moved it.

Juliet stood by my car.

'So you and Nick are friends,' I said to her. 'You didn't tell me about that.'

Juliet said nothing for a minute. 'You don't understand,' she said in the end. 'It's very difficult.'

I drove back on to the road. I nearly cried, and I felt very angry. Juliet was my friend. I had coffee with her and went to the cinema with her, but she said nothing about Nick. Why not? I had dinner with Nick and we talked all evening, but he said nothing about Juliet. Why not? I felt angry with Juliet and with Nick.

That evening Mrs Harvey's arthritis was bad and she went to bed early. Duncan cooked dinner and I ate with him and the children. Duncan talked and laughed with the children and I felt happy to be with them. Once, I felt

Duncan's eyes on me, and suddenly my face felt hot. I didn't want to think about Juliet and Nick.

But later, in my room, I remembered Juliet's angry face and eyes. *We don't want more accidents. Remember Miranda.* Then I remembered old Mrs Harvey in London. *The children's mother died two years ago.* She told me that, but she didn't tell me about an accident. Perhaps it was a car accident? Perhaps Nick killed Miranda with his Landrover? *Duncan hates Nick.* Mrs Harvey told me that, too. Did Duncan hate Nick because Nick killed Miranda?

I slept in the end, but I didn't sleep well. The next day was Saturday and I was free in the morning. Duncan went to the shops with the children and I went to the library in Cromer. Miranda died on 30th September, two years ago. I knew that. Perhaps the town's newspaper wrote about her after she died. I must find *something* about her because I wanted to understand the Harvey family.

I found the old newspapers and began to read. The newspaper of 1st October told me everything.

YOUNG MOTHER DIES IN TERRIBLE ACCIDENT

Miranda Harvey, aged 26, fell down the stairs at her home and died later in hospital. Miranda lived with her husband and two children not far from Cromer. Duncan Harvey's mother lives with them. 'This is a terrible day for the Harvey family,' she said. 'We all loved Miranda

I could not move.

very much, and now her two little children are without a mother.'

Juliet, aged 24, Miranda's sister, is a teacher at one of the schools in Cromer. 'My sister was a wonderful mother,' she said, 'and a loving sister to me.'

I sat with my head in my hands. I could not move. *We don't want more accidents. Remember Miranda.* It wasn't a car accident; Miranda, that wonderful mother, fell down the stairs at Beach House – and I ran up and down those stairs six or seven times a day.

21

Then I looked at some of the later newspapers.

POLICE QUESTION DUNCAN HARVEY

Harvey, aged 34, was at home on the day of his wife's accident. He was upstairs with her before she fell. Then he went downstairs to the kitchen. How did the accident happen? Harvey does not know. He heard nothing, he says.

The police questioned Duncan for two days, I read, but in the end he went home to his children. It wasn't Nick, in his Landrover. Miranda died at home, and the police questioned Duncan. My hands were cold, my legs were cold, and I felt afraid.

Things were different at Beach House after my visit to the library. The house was a house with a secret, and the Harveys were a family with a secret. I thought about Miranda and the accident every day. I wanted to talk to someone about it, but I was afraid. Why did the police question Duncan? *Be careful at Beach House.* Why did Nick say that to me? Was it because of Miranda's accident? There were more questions in my head now. And the biggest question was this: did Miranda fall – or did someone push her?

4

Not one of the family

Winter came. The weather was cold and windy, but sometimes when the weather was a little better I walked on the beach with the children. Two or three times I saw Nick and he smiled and we talked a little. I liked Nick, but I was angry with him because of Juliet, and he didn't ask me to dinner again.

School finished for Christmas, and I drove the children to a farm near Cromer to buy a Christmas tree. After my mother and father died, Christmas was a bad time for me because I was lonely. 'But this year,' I thought, 'I'm going to be with the Harvey family. Perhaps I can forget about Miranda's accident and feel happy at Christmas.'

'Christmas is coming! Christmas is coming!' the children sang. They were very happy about Christmas.

We walked through the farm and looked at the Christmas trees. Tim ran up and down. 'I want this tree, Cathy!' he called. Then he ran up and down again. 'I want this tree, Cathy!' he called again.

Suddenly he ran into a tree and then fell over. When he fell, his head hit a second tree. He began to cry.

I ran to him. There was a long cut on his head and a lot of blood.

'Don't cry, Tim. You're going to be all right,' I said quietly. 'Let's go to the hospital and see the doctor.'

'Oh no!' cried Susan. 'The hospital! Is Tim going to die?'

'Is Tim going to die?'

'No, no. Tim's going to be all right. But the doctor must look at this cut on his head,' I said. I carried Tim to the car and drove quickly to the hospital. After we saw the doctor, I phoned Duncan and he came to the hospital.

Susan ran to him. 'Daddy, there was an accident, and there was a lot of blood. Is he going to die?'

Duncan sat down. His face was white, but he smiled at Susan and Tim. 'Tim's going to be OK. Look at him! He's feeling much better now.'

Duncan put his arm around me. 'Thank you, Cathy,' he said. 'You're very good with the children. Beach House is a happier home now, with you there.' Slowly we walked out of the hospital. 'Please come home in the car with us,' Duncan said. 'We can come back later for your car. Please.'

I liked Duncan then, and I wanted to go with him and the children. But I was afraid, too, because of Miranda's accident. I didn't want to talk to him, and so I went home in my car.

The next day Juliet came to see Tim. She played with the children and then she stayed for dinner. After the children went to bed, she came to see me in my room.

'I'm sorry, Cathy,' she began. 'I wanted to see you, but I was afraid because you're angry with me.'

'Yes, I am angry,' I said slowly. 'You were my friend. I went to dinner with Nick and I told you everything, but you didn't tell me about you and Nick. Why not?'

Juliet looked at me but said nothing.

'Why didn't Nick tell me about you? Did he tell you about our dinner?'

'Yes. I was upset, but Nick likes to talk to women. He likes you and he wanted to take you to dinner. But he loves me and nothing is going to change that.' She stopped. 'I told Grandma about your dinner with Nick, because I didn't want you to be friends with Nick.'

'You don't want her to know about *you* and Nick, but you told her about my dinner with Nick! Why? I don't understand!'

'I'm sorry. I love him very much; he's everything to me. But our love is a secret. Duncan hates Nick, and I don't want him to know about our love.'

'There are a lot of secrets in this family,' I said. 'Secrets about you and Nick. Secrets about Miranda. Why didn't you tell me about Miranda's accident?'

'How do you know about that?' Juliet asked.

'I went to the library and read about it in the newspapers.'

Juliet stood up. 'Nobody talks about Miranda's accident,' she said. 'Nobody saw her when she fell down the stairs.'

I wanted to ask about Duncan. I wanted to ask: 'Why did the police question Duncan?' but I was afraid of the answer. 'Well, I don't like living with all these secrets,' I

'Why didn't you tell me about Miranda's accident?'

said. 'Every time I go downstairs I remember Miranda.'

Juliet laughed then, and it was a cold laugh. 'We all live with that, Cathy. You're not one of the family; you're not going to fall downstairs.'

* * *

27

Tim felt better the next day, and in the afternoon Duncan took the children back to the farm to buy the Christmas tree. And then I phoned Nick.

'I want to talk to you,' I said quietly. 'I need to talk to someone.'

'Mmm,' said Nick. 'Let's meet on the beach. At three o'clock.'

I waited in my room and listened to the sea and the wind. Perhaps Juliet was with Nick. I didn't know, but I needed to talk to someone about the Harvey family. I walked slowly across the field and down the hill to the beach. It

'Did you tell him to come?'

28

was a cold afternoon and there was a strong wind. The sea was dark. Nick wasn't there; perhaps he didn't want to talk to me. But in the end he arrived.

'What's the matter?' he asked.

'I talked to Juliet last night,' I began. 'About Miranda. I don't know why, but I feel afraid. What do you know about Miranda's accident?'

'The police questioned Duncan,' Nick said. His blue eyes looked past me. Suddenly his face changed. 'Duncan's here. Did you tell him to come?'

29

'No, I didn't. He left the house before I called you.'

Duncan ran down the hill. 'Cathy!' he called.

'What are you doing here?' Nick said angrily. 'Cathy wants to talk to me.'

'Cathy, come home,' Duncan said quietly.

'She's not going back with you. She's afraid of you.'

'Afraid of me? Why?'

I said nothing. Duncan's face was angry.

'Why don't you tell us about Miranda?' Nick asked. His face was angry, too. 'I want to ask you something. The police questioned you, Duncan. What did you tell them about that night?'

'So you're asking me about Miranda,' Duncan shouted. 'You remember Miranda, then? Well, I remember, too. I remember her every day.' Duncan looked at me, and then back at Nick. 'You think I killed Miranda? Go to the police, then, and tell them that. Yes, I hated her, and I hated you, too, Nick. She wanted to leave me and the children because of you. She loved you. She told me that. But did you love her, Nick?'

'Of course I didn't,' Nick said. His face was red. 'I liked Miranda. We went to dinner four or five times, that's all. She was lonely.' He looked at me. His eyes were very blue, but suddenly I didn't like his eyes and I didn't like his face.

'She wanted to leave me and her children, but you didn't love her,' Duncan said. 'You loved her sister. I know that.

30

'You think I killed Miranda?'

But Miranda didn't know about you and Juliet. Why didn't you tell her?'

I didn't want to listen. I felt ill and very cold, and I began to walk back up the hill. I wanted to go home, but where was my home? I didn't have one.

5

Home

'Cathy! Wait for me!' It was Duncan. He ran up behind me. 'I want to talk to you, Cathy. Listen – all women like Nick. I know that. But he's not a good friend for you to have. You heard him on the beach. He likes to have lots of women friends. How can you be happy with a man like that?'

'You're wrong,' I said slowly. 'I stopped liking Nick weeks ago.' Nick wasn't important to me now, I knew that.

'I stopped liking Nick weeks ago.'

32

But Duncan *was* important to me – and I couldn't tell him. For a minute or two I said nothing, but the questions were still there. In the end I said: 'Why didn't you tell me about Miranda's accident? Why was it a secret? I feel very upset about all this.'

'I wanted to forget all about it,' Duncan said slowly. 'It was a very difficult time. Miranda and Juliet loved Nick. Juliet hated Miranda. She was afraid because Miranda wanted to live with Nick. Juliet told me about Miranda and Nick because she wanted me to stop Miranda.'

'Juliet told me about her love for Nick. It was a secret, she said.'

'A secret?' Duncan laughed angrily. 'Well, Miranda never knew about it, it's true. Juliet's very careful – she never talks about Nick. But it wasn't difficult to see. I saw her car at his farm, and I often see it there now.'

The sky was darker now. 'Was Juliet here, the night Miranda died?' I asked. Perhaps Juliet killed her sister, I thought.

'No, no. Juliet wasn't here, Nick wasn't here,' Duncan said. 'I was upstairs, and the children were in bed. Then Miranda called me into our bedroom and said: "I'm going to leave you, Duncan. I'm going to live with Nick." I was very angry and upset, but I ran downstairs into the kitchen before she fell. Cathy, nobody killed Miranda. It was an accident, a terrible accident.' Duncan put his hand on my

'Can't you forget about Miranda now?'

arm. 'Can't you forget about Miranda now? Can't we begin again?'

But I couldn't answer then.

We arrived at Beach House. There was a light downstairs in the kitchen, and a light in the sitting room.

'The children are watching television,' Duncan said. We went into the house and Duncan opened the sitting room door. 'We're home now,' he told the children. 'We're going to the kitchen to make dinner.'

34

The kitchen was warm and quiet. Old Mrs Harvey sat in her chair. Suddenly, I felt afraid again. There was something terrible about old Mrs Harvey's face. I stood by the kitchen door; I couldn't go into the room.

'We're back, Mother,' Duncan said. 'Cathy's with me; everything's all right.'

Mrs Harvey's eyes were dark in her white face. 'I was afraid, Duncan! I was afraid! The children love Cathy, and you love Cathy. I can see that. But Cathy loves Nick. She's

'It's all happening again. I can see that.'

going to leave you and the children. Remember Miranda! It's all happening again. I can see that.'

'Mother! It's not true! Don't talk like this!'

'Remember Miranda!' Mrs Harvey said again. 'Don't be upset, Duncan. I'm always here, you know that. I can't look after you because of my arthritis, but I love you most, you know that, and I'm going to help you again.'

Suddenly I understood it all. 'Tell us about Miranda,' I said quietly. 'What did you do that night?'

Mrs Harvey looked at me then. 'I don't want you to leave, Cathy. I want you to stay with the children and be happy with Duncan. Let me tell you about that night,' she said, 'and then you must stay here with us.'

The room was very quiet. Duncan held my hand, and his hand was warm and strong.

'Miranda wanted to leave Duncan. I was upstairs in my room, and I heard her. Duncan ran downstairs and I came out of my room and talked to Miranda. She hated Duncan, and she didn't want to think about her children.' Mrs Harvey began to cry. 'I pushed her. She was on the stairs, and I pushed her with my stick. She fell down the stairs, and I went back into my room. I didn't want to kill her, I wanted to break her legs. I wanted her to stay at home with Duncan. But she died, and in the end I was happy because she didn't go and live with Nick . . .'

Mrs Harvey talked and talked, and in the end we stopped listening to her.

'Cathy, this is all going to be very difficult,' Duncan said, tiredly. 'I must call the police and tell them about mother. Then I must talk to the children. It's going to be difficult for you, too. Are you going to leave Beach House?'

I smiled. There were no more questions in my head. I knew everything now about the Harvey family: there was

I found my home in his arms.

nothing more to be afraid of. 'No, Duncan, I'm not going to leave.'

'The children need you,' he said. 'You know that. But I need you too. I want you to be with me. But can we be happy after all this?'

'Of course we can,' I told him. 'Things are going to get better now, for all of us.'

He put his arms around me. He kissed me then, and I found my home in his arms.

GLOSSARY

around on all sides
arthritis a painful disease of the joints
beach the sand or stones at the edge of the sea
blood the red liquid in our bodies
company people working together for money
cook to heat food
cut *(n)* an opening made by something sharp
dear (**my dear**) a much loved person
fall (past tense **fell**) to go down suddenly
farm *(n)* land and buildings where people grow things and
   keep animals for food
field a piece of land with a fence or hedge round it
hate to dislike someone very much: opposite of 'to love'
immediately at once
job when you work and get money for it, you have a job
kind friendly and helpful
kiss *(v)* to touch someone with the lips to show love
kitchen a room where people cook
Landrover a car useful for travelling on rough roads
library a building where books and newspapers are kept
light something that makes a room bright, not dark
lonely without friends
look after to make someone happy and comfortable
newspaper a paper giving news every day
push to press against something and make it move suddenly
school a place where children go every day to learn
secret something you do not want anyone else to know
shout to talk very loudly

stick   a long thin piece of wood; it can help an old person to
   walk

strong   powerful; not easily hurt

terrible   very bad

upset   worried and sad

wind *(n)*   air moving quickly and strongly

Remember Miranda

ACTIVITIES

ACTIVITIES

Before Reading

1 **Read the back cover of the book. How much do you know now about the story? Tick one box for each sentence.**

	YES	NO	PERHAPS
1 Cathy Wilson is going to begin a new job.	☐	☐	☐
2 There are three children in the Harvey family.	☐	☐	☐
3 Cathy likes Nick, the farmer.	☐	☐	☐
4 The children's mother was called Miranda.	☐	☐	☐
5 The children's mother died a month ago.	☐	☐	☐
6 Everybody talks about Miranda.	☐	☐	☐
7 Cathy is beautiful.	☐	☐	☐

2 **Now read the story introduction on the first page of the book, and choose the best ending for these sentences.**

1 Cathy's parents . . .
   a) live in Norfolk.
   b) are very old.
   c) live with the Harvey family.
   d) are dead.

2 Cathy is sometimes lonely because . . .

   a) this is her first job.

   b) she doesn't like the children.

   c) she has no friends.

   d) Mrs Harvey is old.

3 After Cathy has dinner with Nick, . . .

   a) Mrs Harvey gets angry.

   b) Duncan goes to London.

   c) she hates Duncan.

   d) she leaves Beach House.

3 **Why does everybody remember Miranda? Can you guess? Here are some possible answers.**
Tick one box for each answer.

	YES	NO
Everybody remembers Miranda because . . .		
1 she was very beautiful.	☐	☐
2 she was very kind and loving.	☐	☐
3 everybody hated her.	☐	☐
4 everybody loved her.	☐	☐
5 she did something terrible.	☐	☐
6 she was a bad mother.	☐	☐

ACTIVITIES

While Reading

Read Chapter 1. Choose the best question-word, and then answer the questions.

Who / Why

1 . . . did Cathy arrive late at Beach House?
2 . . . did Cathy meet on the sea road in Cromer?
3 . . . was Duncan Harvey angry?
4 . . . was Juliet?
5 . . . did Cathy meet one day in Cromer?
6 . . . did Juliet often visit Miranda?

Read Chapter 2. Who said this, and to whom?

1 'Be careful at Beach House.'
2 'Why don't you like Duncan?'
3 'I don't want you to see Nick again.'
4 'Why are you afraid of Nick?'
5 'He's a bad man. Grandma told me.'

Read Chapter 3. Here are some untrue sentences about the chapter. Change them into true sentences.

1 Duncan never drove the children to school.
2 Nick's Landrover hit Cathy's car.

Idea Store Bow

Customer ID: ******8203

Items that you have renewed

Title: Remember Miranda
ID: 91000004133229
Due: 12 June 2021

Title: The piano man
ID: 91000004332086
Due: 12 June 2021

Total items: 2
Account balance: £0.00
22/05/2021 15:22
Borrowed: 2
Overdue: 0
Hold requests: 0
Ready for collection: 0

24 hour renewal line: 0333 370 4700
www.ideastore.co.uk

3 Cathy knew about Juliet and Nick.
4 Cathy learnt about Miranda's accident from the police.
5 Miranda died in a car accident.
6 Duncan Harvey was away on the day of his wife's accident.

Read Chapter 4, and then answer these questions.

Who
1 . . . ran into a tree and then fell over?
2 . . . was afraid of Duncan because of Miranda's accident?
3 . . . told Grandma about Cathy's dinner with Nick?
4 . . . hated Miranda and hated Nick, too?
5 . . . liked Miranda, but didn't love her?
6 . . . wanted to leave Duncan?

Before you read Chapter 5, look at these questions. Can you guess the best answers?

1 Who killed Miranda?
   a) Juliet   c) Duncan
   b) Mrs Harvey   d) Nobody
2 What happens to Cathy? She . . .
   a) leaves Beach House.   c) goes to live with Nick.
   b) finds a home.   d) learns all the secrets of the Harvey family.

After Reading

1 Match the people with the sentences. Then use the sentences to write about the people. Use pronouns (*he, she*) and linking words (*and, but*).

Cathy / Juliet / Mrs Harvey / Nick / Miranda / Duncan

Example: *Cathy works at Beach House. She looks after Susan and Tim, **but she** . . .*

  1 *Cathy* works at Beach House.
  2 _____ was Miranda's sister.
  3 _____ has arthritis.
  4 _____ is tall with blue eyes.
  5 _____ died two years ago.
  6 _____ has a job with a big London company.
  7 _____ lives in a farm near Beach House.
  8 *Cathy* looks after Susan and Tim.
  9 _____ works as a teacher.
 10 _____ plays with his children every day.
 11 _____ is lonely because she has no friends.
 12 _____ likes to have lots of women friends.
 13 _____ loved her children.
 14 _____ is kind to his mother.
 15 _____ walks with a stick.

16 _____ loves Nick very much.

17 _____ wanted to leave Duncan because she loved Nick.

18 _____ often feels upset because she can't look after the children.

2 **Before Miranda died, Juliet talked to Duncan (see page 33). Use these words to complete their conversation. (Use each word once.)**

about, and, because, before, but, friendly, happy, lonely, often, telling, told, true, upset, want

DUNCAN: What's the matter, Juliet? You look _____.

JULIET: I *am* upset! I want to talk to you _____ Miranda.

DUNCAN: Miranda's not _____. I know that. She's lonely _____ I often work in London.

JULIET: Well, she's not _____ now. She's very _____ with Nick.

DUNCAN: Nick? But you're Nick's girlfriend! I _____ see your car at his farm.

JULIET: Yes, I know, _____ that doesn't stop Miranda. She loves Nick _____ she wants to live with him.

DUNCAN: What?! No, no, that's not _____!

JULIET: Oh yes it is! She _____ me yesterday.

DUNCAN: And why are you _____ me?

JULIET: Because I _____ you to stop her, Duncan! Talk to her. Talk to her soon, _____ she leaves you and the children.

3 Here is a new illustration for the story. Find the best place in the story to put the picture, and answer these questions.

The picture goes on page _____.

1 Who are the two women in this picture?

2 Where are Duncan and the children at this moment?

3 What happened next?

Now write a caption for the illustration.

Caption: _____

4 **After the end of the story, Juliet came to see Duncan and Cathy. Their conversation is in the wrong order. Write it out in the correct order and put in the speakers' names.**

1 _____ 'Tell them what? She told them everything two years ago.'

2 _____ 'Yes, she loved her. But Mother didn't want Miranda to leave me and the children.'

3 _____ 'I don't believe it! Grandma loved my sister!'

4 _____ 'Duncan called the police. His mother wanted to tell them something about Miranda's accident.'

5 _____ 'What happened yesterday? Nick phoned me. He saw the police here.'

6 _____ 'Well, not everything. You see, Mother killed Miranda. She pushed her down the stairs.'

5 **What happened next? Finish Cathy's story for her, with the words and names below. (Use some more than once.)**

Juliet, Duncan, Nick, Mrs Harvey, the children, the police, him, her, she, we, I, us

_____ came and took _____ away. Later, _____ went to live in a hospital. _____ stayed at Beach House with _____. _____ are very happy, and now _____ have a new mother. _____ and _____ are good friends, and _____ often visits _____. And what about _____ at the farm? Well, perhaps _____ visits _____ sometimes, but that's _____ secret.

ABOUT THE AUTHOR

Rowena Akinyemi is British, and after many years in Africa, she now lives and works in Cambridge. She has worked in English Language Teaching for twenty years, in Africa and England, and has been writing ELT fiction for ten years. She has written several other stories for the Oxford Bookworms Library, including *Love or Money?* and *The Witches of Pendle* (both at Stage 1). She has also written books for children. This story, *Remember Miranda*, was inspired by family holidays on the Norfolk coast.

OXFORD BOOKWORMS LIBRARY

Classics • Crime & Mystery • Factfiles • Fantasy & Horror
Human Interest • Playscripts • Thriller & Adventure
True Stories • World Stories

The OXFORD BOOKWORMS LIBRARY provides enjoyable reading in English, with a wide range of classic and modern fiction, non-fiction, and plays. It includes original and adapted texts in seven carefully graded language stages, which take learners from beginner to advanced level. An overview is given on the next pages.

All Stage 1 titles are available as audio recordings, as well as over eighty other titles from Starter to Stage 6. All Starters and many titles at Stages 1 to 4 are specially recommended for younger learners. Every Bookworm is illustrated, and Starters and Factfiles have full-colour illustrations.

The OXFORD BOOKWORMS LIBRARY also offers extensive support. Each book contains an introduction to the story, notes about the author, a glossary, and activities. Additional resources include tests and worksheets, and answers for these and for the activities in the books. There is advice on running a class library, using audio recordings, and the many ways of using Oxford Bookworms in reading programmes. Resource materials are available on the website <www.oup.com/bookworms>.

The *Oxford Bookworms Collection* is a series for advanced learners. It consists of volumes of short stories by well-known authors, both classic and modern. Texts are not abridged or adapted in any way, but carefully selected to be accessible to the advanced student.

You can find details and a full list of titles in the *Oxford Bookworms Library Catalogue* and *Oxford English Language Teaching Catalogues*, and on the website <www.oup.com/bookworms>.

THE OXFORD BOOKWORMS LIBRARY
GRADING AND SAMPLE EXTRACTS

STARTER • 250 HEADWORDS

present simple – present continuous – imperative –
can/cannot, must – *going to* (future) – simple gerunds …

Her phone is ringing – but where is it?

Sally gets out of bed and looks in her bag. No phone. She looks under the bed. No phone. Then she looks behind the door. There is her phone. Sally picks up her phone and answers it. *Sally's Phone*

STAGE 1 • 400 HEADWORDS

… past simple – coordination with *and, but, or* –
subordination with *before, after, when, because, so* …

I knew him in Persia. He was a famous builder and I worked with him there. For a time I was his friend, but not for long. When he came to Paris, I came after him – I wanted to watch him. He was a very clever, very dangerous man. *The Phantom of the Opera*

STAGE 2 • 700 HEADWORDS

… present perfect – *will* (future) – *(don't) have to, must not, could* –
comparison of adjectives – simple *if* clauses – past continuous –
tag questions – *ask/tell* + infinitive …

While I was writing these words in my diary, I decided what to do. I must try to escape. I shall try to get down the wall outside. The window is high above the ground, but I have to try. I shall take some of the gold with me – if I escape, perhaps it will be helpful later. *Dracula*

STAGE 3 • 1000 HEADWORDS

... should, may – present perfect continuous – *used to* – past perfect –
causative – relative clauses – indirect statements ...

Of course, it was most important that no one should see
Colin, Mary, or Dickon entering the secret garden. So Colin
gave orders to the gardeners that they must all keep away
from that part of the garden in future. ***The Secret Garden***

STAGE 4 • 1400 HEADWORDS

... past perfect continuous – passive (simple forms) –
would conditional clauses – indirect questions –
relatives with *where/when* – gerunds after prepositions/phrases ...

I was glad. Now Hyde could not show his face to the world
again. If he did, every honest man in London would be proud
to report him to the police. ***Dr Jekyll and Mr Hyde***

STAGE 5 • 1800 HEADWORDS

... future continuous – future perfect –
passive (modals, continuous forms) –
would have conditional clauses – modals + perfect infinitive ...

If he had spoken Estella's name, I would have hit him. I was so
angry with him, and so depressed about my future, that I could
not eat the breakfast. Instead I went straight to the old house.
Great Expectations

STAGE 6 • 2500 HEADWORDS

... passive (infinitives, gerunds) – advanced modal meanings –
clauses of concession, condition

When I stepped up to the piano, I was confident. It was as if I
knew that the prodigy side of me really did exist. And when I
started to play, I was so caught up in how lovely I looked that
I didn't worry how I would sound. ***The Joy Luck Club***

The Omega Files – Short Stories

JENNIFER BASSETT

In EDI (the European Department of Intelligence in Brussels) there are some very secret files – the Omega Files. There are strange, surprising, and sometimes horrible stories in these files, but not many people know about them. You never read about them in the newspapers.

Hawker and Jude know all about the Omega Files, because they work for EDI. They think fast, they move fast, and they learn some very strange things. They go all over the world, asking difficult questions in dangerous places, but they don't always find the answers . . .

BOOKWORMS · CRIME & MYSTERY · STAGE 1

Sherlock Holmes and the Sport of Kings

SIR ARTHUR CONAN DOYLE

Retold by Jennifer Bassett

Horseracing is the sport of kings, perhaps because racehorses are very expensive animals. But when they win races, they can make a lot of money too – money for the owners, for the trainers, and for the people who put bets on them to win.

Silver Blaze is a young horse, but already the winner of many races. One night he disappears from his stables, and someone kills his trainer. The police want the killer, and the owner wants his horse, but they can't find them. So what do they do?

They write to 221B Baker Street, London, of course – to ask for the help of the great detective, Sherlock Holmes.